Confession of Sin

&

Freedom from it

*Breaking bad habits
& destructive addictions
by coming to terms with
Redemption realities!*

Rudi Louw

Copyright © 2014 Rudi Louw Publishing

All rights reserved solely by the author. No part of this book may be reproduced in any form *without the permission of the author.*

Scripture quotations are mostly from the *New King James Version,* Holy Bible, Thomas Nelson Publishers, Copyright © 1983 by Thomas Nelson, Inc.

Scripture quotations not taken from the NKJV or Mirror Bible *are a literal translation of the Scriptures.*

The Holy Scriptures are just that, HOLY.

Statements enclosed in brackets were inserted into Scripture quotations, to add emphasis or to clarify the meaning of what is being said in those scriptures. The integrity of God's Word to Man was not compromised in any way. Due care and diligence was cautiously exercised to keep the Word of Truth intact.

For example, the apostle Paul said in his second letter to Timothy in chapter three verse sixteen that: *"All Scripture is given by inspiration of God* (literally God breathed)*, and is profitable for doctrine, for reproof, for correction, for instruction **in righteousness**,"*

Table of Contents

The Marvel of the Holy Bible 5
Acknowledgment 11
Foreword 13
Introduction 17
1. *The Eternal New Testament Perspective!* 33
2. *Not an Inferior Redemption* 47
3. *Faith's Confession* 51
4. *Addiction* 69
5. *Freedom Realized!* 79
About The Author 93

The Marvel of the Holy Bible

1. Uninterrupted Theme and Inspired Thought

It took *1,500 years* to compile the Holy Bible, involving *more than 40 different authors*. <u>Yet</u> the theme and inspired thought of Scripture continues *uninterrupted* from author to author, from beginning till end.

2. Absence of Mythical Stories

Compare philosophies and theories about creation in the Middle East, Europe, Asia, Africa, and Latin America and you'll find mythical scenarios: gods feuding and cutting up other gods to form the heavens and the earth, etc.

In ancient Greek mythology, the Greeks see Atlas carrying the earth on his shoulders. In India, Hindus believe eight elephants carry the earth on their backs.

But in contrast, Job, the oldest book in the Holy Bible, declares that, *"God suspends the earth on nothing."* (Job 26:7)

This was said millennia before Isaac Newton discovered the invisible laws of gravity that delicately balance every planet and sun in its individual circuit.

Contrary to every other ancient attempt to give a creation account, *the Holy Bible pictures the creation of the earth in a very scientific manner.*

For example, in Genesis Chapter One, the continents are lifted from the seas, then vegetation is formed and later animal life, all reproducing *'according to its own kind'*, **thus recognizing the fixed genetic laws.** In addition, we have the bringing forth of man and woman, *all done by God in a dignified and proper manner, without mythological adornments.*

The balance or remainder of the Holy Bible follows suite.

The narratives are **true historical documents**, *faithfully reflecting society and culture* **as history and archaeology would discover them thousands of years later. Not only is the Holy Bible historically accurate, it is also reliable when it deals with scientifically provable subjects.**

It was never intended to be a textbook on history, science, mathematics, or medicine. *However, when its writers touch on these subjects,* **they often state facts that scientific advancement would not reveal, or even consider, until thousands of years later.**

While many have doubted the accuracy of the Holy Bible, time and continued research have consistently demonstrated that the Word of God is better informed than its critics.

3. Intactness

Of all the ancient works of substantial size, *the Holy Bible survives intact, against all odds and expectations.*

Compared with other ancient writings, the Holy Bible has more manuscripts as evidence to support it than any ten pieces of classical literature combined!

The plays of William Shakespeare, for instance, were written about four hundred years ago, after the invention of the printing press. Many of his original writings and words have been lost in numerous sections, *yet the Holy Bible's uncanny preservation has weathered thousands of years of wars, contradictions, persecutions, fires and invasions.*

Through the centuries Jewish scribes have preserved the Holy Bible's Old Covenant text, **such as no other manuscripts have ever been preserved. They kept tabs on every letter, syllable, word and paragraph.** *They continued from generation to generation to appoint and train special groups of men within their culture* **whose sole duty it was to preserve and transmit these documents <u>with perfect accuracy and fidelity</u>.**

Who ever bothered to count the letters, syllables, or words of Plato, Aristotle, or Seneca for that matter?

When it comes to the New Testament, the actual number of preserved manuscripts is so great that it becomes overwhelming. **There are more than 5,680 Greek manuscripts, more than 10,000 Latin Vulgate manuscripts and at least 9,300 other versions. Further still, there exists an additional 25,000 manuscript copies of portions of the New Testament.** No other document of antiquity even begins to approach such numbers.

The closest in comparison is Homer's <u>Iliad</u>, with only 643 manuscripts. The first complete work of Homer only dates back to the 13th century.

4. Unmatched Accuracy in Predictive Foretelling

The Holy Bible is unmatched in accuracy in predictive foretelling. No other ancient work succeeds in this, or even begins to attempt this.

Other books such as the Koran, the Book of Mormon, and parts of the Veda claim divine inspiration; ***but none of these books contain predictive foretelling.***

This one undeniable fact we know for certain: *While microscopic scrutiny would show up the imperfections, blemishes, and defects of any work of Man, <u>it magnifies the beauties and perfection of God</u>. Just as every flower displays in accurate detail the reflection and perfection of beauty, <u>so does the Word of Truth when it is scrutinized</u>.*

Historian Philip Schaff wrote:

"Without money and weapons, Jesus the Christ conquered more millions than Alexander, Caesar, Mohammad, and Napoleon. Without science and learning, He (Jesus the Christ) shed more light on things human and divine than all philosophers and scholars combined. Without the eloquence of schools, He (Jesus the Christ) spoke such words of life as was never spoken before or since and produced effects which lie beyond the reach of orator or poet. Without writing a single line, He (Jesus the Christ) set more pens in motion and furnished themes for more

sermons, orations, discussions, learned volumes, works of art, and songs of praise **than the whole army of great men of ancient and modern times combined**." (The Person of Christ, p33. 1913)

Today, there are literally billions of Bibles in more than 2,000 languages.

Isn't it about time you find out what it really has to say?

Hey listen, the Holy Bible is all about Jesus, the Messiah, the Christ…

…and everything about Jesus Christ is really about YOU!!

Study Tips:

Read 2 Corinthians 5:14, 16, 18, 19, and 21.

In the light of these Scriptures, it should be obvious that, if you want to study the Holy Bible, *you should study it in the light of Mankind's redemption!*

Feed daily on redemption realities found in the book of Acts, in Romans Chapters One through Eight, and in Ephesians, Colossians, and Galatians. These realities may also be found in 1 Peter Chapter One, 2 Peter Chapter One, James Chapter 1, as well as in 1 and 2 Corinthians.

Acknowledgment

I want to acknowledge and thank one of my mentors in the faith, Francois du Toit, for blessing and impacting my life with revelation knowledge.

The portion on *"The Marvel of the Holy Bible"* was borrowed from his website, http://www.MirrorWord.net/, as students so often feel they have a right to do with things that come from teachers they respect. Just as Galatians 6:6 says, *"Let him who is taught the Word **share in all good things** with him who teaches."*

I also want to say a special thank you to the person who may have first preached the majority of what I wrote about in this book, *even though I do not remember who you are or where I got your teaching from now over 20 years ago already.* Please know that it made such an impact on my life and set me free and totally changed my relationship with Father God! Thank you!

I also want to acknowledge my very dear friends, Andre & Mary-Anne Rabe, *whom I also quote in this book.*

Thank you for tirelessly and gently preaching and teaching the beautiful truth of the gospel everywhere you go with such simplicity and clarity. You are truly helping many people get free by your simple but profound message! I love you guys!

To all our other many dear friends and family, *and to Chase Aderhold and all those who helped me with this project,*

...but especially to my sweet wife Carmen:

For all your love and support,

THANK YOU!

I LOVE YOU!

Foreword

Thank you for taking the time to read this book.

Let me start off by saying that *I am totally addicted to my Daddy's love for me.*

I am in love with Jesus Christ, *and that is enough for me!*

The love of God is so much more than a doctrine, a philosophy, or a theory. It is so much more and goes so much deeper than knowledge; it way surpasses knowledge. *We are talking heart language here.*

I write *to impact people's hearts;* to make them see the mysteries that have been hidden in Father God's heart concerning Christ Jesus, and really *concerning THEM,* so as to arrest their conscience with it, that *I may introduce them to their original design, and to their true selves;* **and present them to themselves perfect in Christ Jesus**, *and set them apart unto Him **in love**,* as a chaste virgin,

We are involved with the biggest romance of the ages. Therefore this book cannot be read as you would a novel; *casually.* It is not a cleverly devised little myth or fable. **It contains revelation and *truth* into some**

things you may or may not have considered before.

It is not blasphemy or error though. ***It is the TRUTH of God, ultimate TRUTH, and therefore, has direct bearing upon YOUR life.*** **The Word and the Spirit is my witness** *to the reality of these things!*

Be like the people of Berea the apostle Paul ministered to in Acts 17:11. Open yourself up to study the revelation contained in this book *to discover for yourself the reality of these things.*

But be forewarned! Do not become guilty of the sins of the Pharisees, ***or you too will miss out on the depth of fulfillment God Himself, who is LOVE, wants to give you.***

Jesus said of the Pharisees and Sadducees that they strain out every little gnat, BUT swallow whole camels. What He meant by that is that *some people seem to have it all together when it comes to doctrine, and they love to argue.* ***It makes them feel important, but it is nothing other than EMPTY religious and intellectual pride.*** *They know the Scriptures in and out, and YET they are still so IGNORANT about* ***REAL TRUTH that is only found in LOVE.*** *They are still so ignorant and indifferent* ***towards the things that REALLY MATTER.*** They are always arguing over the use of *every little jot and tittle* and over the meaning and interpretation of *every word of Scripture.*

The exact thing they accuse everyone else of doing though, the precise thing they judge everyone else for, *they are actually doing themselves.* That is: **they often downright misinterpret and twist what is being said, *making a big deal of insignificant things while obscuring or weakening God's real truth: the truth of His LOVE.*** *They are always majoring on minors,* <u>**because they do not understand the heart of God**</u> *and therefore, they constantly miss the whole point of the message.*

Paul himself said it so beautifully,

*"…the letter kills but **the Spirit BRINGS LIFE**;"*

*"…<u>knowledge puffs up</u>, but **LOVE EDIFIES**."*

I say again:

Allow yourself to get caught up in the revelation I am about to share. Open yourself up to study the insight contained in this book, *not only with a desire to gain knowledge, but also with anticipation **to hear from Father God yourself**;*

*…**to encounter Him through His Word;***

*…**and to embrace truth, in order to know and believe the LOVE God has for <u>you</u>,*** so

that you may get so caught up in it, ***that you too may receive from Him; LOVES' impartation of LIFE.***

This revelation contains within it the voice and call of LOVE Himself to every human being on the face of this earth. *If you take heed to it, it is custom designed and guaranteed to forever alter and enrich your life!*

Introduction

As an introduction to our subject in this book, the following thoughts were mostly taken from my friend Andre Rabe's book, Imagine, then modified and rearranged before being added to my thoughts.

In speaking about the eternal, timeless realm in which God dwells, we should not really use our time related terms and tenses. **Eternity has its own language, and it is different from the language of time!**

When we speak of the eternal timeless realm, we speak about a realm decidedly different from what we normally experience in this physical world.

In time, things decay. In eternity, there is no decay. In time, there is past, present, and future. In timeless eternity, there is no past or future as we observe it in our world, only something similar to what we call the present.

Time began. Eternity is.

Time is often defined as a sequence of events. There certainly are also events in eternity, as seen from 2 Timothy 1:9, but these events are not bound to the past or the future. If there is a sequence, it is based on the significance of the event rather than *'time.'*

While thinking with a mind bound to time, **it is difficult to grasp eternal truth, or eternal reality. It is a different language!**

It takes revelation to see things from God's eternal perspective instead of seeing from a time-bondage perspective.

Only the Holy Spirit can open our eyes to the Father's eternal perspective.

In short, in order for us to comprehend timeless eternity and to understand its language, it will take an impartation of insight and revelation into the knowledge of God by the Holy Spirit Himself.

It is the revelation which comes from Him alone that saves us and lifts us out of our time-bound thinking and a time-bound mentality.

We exist within the context of time. Even our language is mostly bound to time. But God wants us to understand and communicate freely in His language, in the language of that eternal spirit realm, of that eternal spirit truth, that eternal spirit reality.

Life is like a massive movie that we joined halfway through the screening. Just imagine walking into a cinema, half-way through the film. It will probably take you a while to figure out the plot and to understand the characters, having missed the beginning.

You see, we have all entered a story that began long before we were born. We are part of a very-very big story, written by God Himself. **This story began before creation.**

Although we, you and I entered this story rather late, the Director wants to let us in on the whole story **so we can understand our importance and become a significant part of the story**.

The secret of understanding this story and being able to speak its language and communicate its plot from beginning to end is not out of reach to any one of us. God has placed that language, He has placed eternity into our hearts so that we too can have access into those realms of timeless eternity, beyond the here and now of our existence. (Read Ecclesiastes 3:11, 2 Timothy 1:9, and Ephesians 1:4 & 5)

So, in God, there exists a timeless realm not subject to decay, a spirit realm of spiritual reality; a realm of Spirit Truth.

What happens in that timeless realm is immutable. What is declared in that realm is unchangeable and what is given to us in that realm is irreversible, *"for God's gifts and His call are irrevocable."* (Romans 11:29. Read also Isaiah 46:10)

When John writes about the Word that was in the beginning (John 1:1), he refers to this eternal, timeless realm of God. He refers to an eternal event, to a decision and forever unchangeable decree that was made in God, concerning us, in that eternal, timeless realm. He refers to an eternal reality, to something much greater than a time-related event.

The word he uses is *'ar-khay'* which means chief (in various applications of order, time, place, or rank), beginning, first (estate), magistrate, power, principality, principle, and rule. **So he speaks of that which is most important, most significant, and most central.**

John is referring to the beginning of all beginnings, the origin of all origins, the first cause, and the very essence of God's motivation.

We are talking about an eternal, timeless event, an event that is forever valid, forever present!

God's eternal motivation, His choice and decree, is new every morning. It is as vibrant, real, urgent, and every bit as true and inspiring, and truth, right now as it has always been.

The incarnation, life, death, and resurrection of Jesus Christ happened within our time, but it was and is a manifestation of an eternal event, an eternal reality and truth within God.

His appearance revealed what has always been true. The exact mystery hidden in the heart of God for ages and generations was and is finally made known in our dimension of time and space.

The message of Christ is nothing less than the unveiling of God's reality, the truth as He sees it.

We can no longer think of God apart from His revelation of Himself in this event. Neither can we think of ourselves apart from God's revelation of us in this event.

God bound Himself inseparably to us. And when the Creator became part of creation, He confirmed it.

Our very existence in this time-bound dimension was forever challenged and altered by this act, by this event that took place in the fullness of time or also known as the end of time.

You see, time itself as a whole has been redeemed, *as God and Man is revealed face to face in the man Jesus Christ,* who is then also resurrected from the dead and eternally raised up, seated as the right hand of God, seated in the eternal spirit realm of spiritual reality and eternal truth.

He is eternally present, the new and yet old, but newly revealed **reality of our existence!**

He is the ultimate representation of the reality of God, and the ultimate representation of the reality of Man.

What He accomplished, what He revealed and then reaffirmed in the work of redemption, can mean nothing less than the total reconciliation of God and Man.

You were in Christ, you were therefore also in His death, in His resurrection, and in His ascension, **because of that timeless eternal association and connection from before time began.**

In Christ you are confronted with the reality of your eternal identity in God, and with the reality of your salvation in every way from a time-bound mentality and existence.

We can do nothing against this truth, only for this truth!

To have faith is to consistently live in the awareness of what God is aware of. Faith is not something we generate ourselves.

The truth and faith of God is contained within the declaration of this eternal gospel. **We can receive it or reject it, but we can never invalidate it or replace it with our own persuasions and perspective. It is a timeless and eternal language with an eternal perspective.**

If it seems that some Scriptures contradict this eternal perspective from which I often write, and from which I wrote this book, it is only because, quite often, the only way God can communicate with natural-minded and fall-minded and law-minded people is through that language which they understand, a time-bound, law-bound, fall-of-Adam-bound language.

For instance, when God addresses the Hebrew mind, He uses the sacrificial system and law-bound language in order to communicate and relate to the Jews.

Even in the New Testament, even in the book of Hebrews, He explains Christ to them from that time and law-bound perspective, in law-bound, time-bound language they can relate to, just in order to get them to understand eternal realities.

In many places in Scripture, He talks about cleansing His own mind by blotting out sin and remembering it no more.

Yet in the eternal realm, God's mind remained cleansed in spite of the fall, because as far as that timeless, eternal realm is concerned, the Lamb (Christ) was slain from before time began. And God, who sees the end from the beginning and lives outside of time, had already made His mind up about Man and had chosen to love Man.

God's truth is eternal, and thus He has never been confused or needs to repent and change His mind or cleanse His mind from anything.

God is not a man that He should be taken off guard and have to adjust His perspective just a little bit. He is not time-bound like us, whom often unexpectedly find out that we have believed a lie, or a half-truth, and that we have been deceived.

"God is light and in Him is no darkness at all."

"He is not a man that He should lie; nor is He a son of man that He should repent."

Our whole identity and our whole existence, our eternal identity and existence are defined in Christ and by Christ, before and after the work of redemption.

In Him all things find their meaning. **The total summary and conclusion of Man's identity and worth is found in Him. He was and is now again after His ascension, forever seated and at rest in this reality!**

We are included in Him and seated with Him – we no longer have to live within the contradiction to eternal reality which entered the world through Adam. For we have an origin that began before Adam **and was revealed and totally restored in Christ to the fullness of its glory.**

Let me just add this one more thing before I get condemned and stoned, just as Stephen was, by law-minded people trapped in a time-bound existence and definition of life.

We are often asked two hugely pertinent questions:

What does it mean to be "in" Christ?

And does it even matter what we believe?

It is obvious they misunderstand what we teach because of their traditional religious teachings and understanding.

Here is our answer:

If by "in" Christ we mean that Christ is the One who gives life and breath to everyone (*"He Himself gives to all men, life, breath, and all other things."* Acts 17:25),

Then YES, in that context, we believe He is present everywhere.

If by "in" Christ we mean that nothing can exist without Him, then YES, we believe He sustains everything, the whole universe!

However, and listen carefully now…

If by "in" Christ we mean a living relationship, a living union between Christ and a person whereby Christ can express Himself through that person;

…**then NO, we don't believe Christ is in everyone, in this context.**

Darkness cannot fellowship with light!

What a person believes absolutely matters!

Faith releases the benefit of the truth. (Hebrews 4:2).

This *"Word of Truth"*, this *"Gospel of Your Salvation"*, **is first and foremost a declaration of the truth as God knows it. It is the declaration of His persuasion.**

In it you are confronted with the reality of your salvation in Christ Jesus.

When you and I are presented with the reality of what God has to say about our timeless, eternal identity in Him, and with what He has done for and with us in Christ to restore us fully to that timeless eternal identity, **it does not remove the need for faith; in fact, IT GREATLY INTENSIFIES IT!**

When we see the **GREATER reality** of God's opinion and truth about us and what He has done for us and to us, to restore us, and how it contrasts with the **LESSER reality** of our experience, **it creates a clear confrontation.**

Do we want to live in God's reality revealed, or continue in the chaos and deception of our own opinions?

Once we've seen God's eternal, timeless truth about ourselves, we cannot reject it without rejecting our own existence.

He chose us and demonstrated His choice of us in Christ beyond doubt.

How can we do anything but make a decision for Him, when we realize His decision for us!

His decision was to give Himself to us completely and to lavish His love upon us all!

In becoming a man He made known that His will and purpose have forever been and will forever be **to be totally united with Man!**

It is on the basis of this decision of God, already made before the ages about us, and made known in time, in Christ, to us, **that we are enabled to make a decision for Him.**

Seeing people come into a living relationship with Christ through the declaration of this eternal good news is the greatest privilege there is!

"Eye has not seen,
nor ear heard,
nor have entered into the heart of Man

**the things which God has prepared
for those who love Him.**

Now we have received,

not the spirit of the world,

but **the Spirit who is from God,**

*that we might know the things
that have been freely given to us by God."*

These things **we also impart**,

not in words which Man's wisdom teaches

but **with words** which the Holy Spirit teaches,

combining Spirit with spirit.

For who has known the mind of the Lord so as to be knitted together with Him? But we have the mind of Christ"

~ 1 Corinthians 2:9 -16

Chapter 1

The Eternal New Testament Perspective!

So many people get so entangled with 1 John 1:9 that they can't fully enter into what the *"the word of Faith"* reveals.

1 John 1:9 says,

*"If we **CONFESS** our sins, He is faithful and just to forgive us our sins **and to cleanse us** from **all un-righteousness**."*

People are so used to reading this Scripture in a religious, legalistic way that they have come to think that, *'**Maybe if we confess our disease enough we'll get healed.**'*

But the truth is, *confessing HIS PROVISION is what gets you healed.*

It's when you begin to confess His provision for sin that you get free from its power and guilt.

Listen, we can never make a doctrine out of just one Scripture; even more so when we isolate it and take it out of context!

I am telling you now: **THE CONTINUAL CONFESSION OF SINS is just as much an ARCHAIC and OUTDATED a practice as THE CONTINUAL OFFERING OF BULLS, SHEEP, and PIGIONS,** *and whatever else.*

THE CONTINUAL CONFESSION OF SINS is a practice that belongs with the OLD, TEMPORARY HEBREW COVENANT and the priesthood of Aaron and Levi, and therefore IT IS NOW AN OUTDATED AND A TOTALLY *UNSCRIPTURAL* **PRACTICE ACCORDING TO THE NEW TESTAMENT!**

The NEW TESTAMENT Scriptures QUITE CLEARLY *do not teach such a practice!*

According to the NEW TESTAMENT Scriptures, Jesus came and did away with the Old, TEMPORARY HEBREW Covenant with its CONTINUAL SACRIFICE SYSTEM and came and established the NEW COVENANT IN HIS BLOOD, the NEW TESTAMENT!

You see, the Levitical priesthood and THAT WHOLE OLD ORDER of service under Aaron and Moses was DONE AWAY WITH and REPLACED by a new and better priestly order, *the new order of Christ. He is our High Priest forever, according to the order of Melchizedek,* <u>*not Levi*</u>*.*

His mediation for us *was every bit as eternal as He is!*

According to the NEW TESTAMENT, *NEITHER FEELING OF REGRET, NOR SORROW,* BUT <u>FAITH</u> IN THE FINISHED WORK OF JESUS <u>IS THE ONLY</u> <u>GROUNDS</u> FOR FORGIVENESS of sins.

Why can I make such a bold statement?

Because Hebrews 9:22 says that,

*"Indeed, under the Law, almost everything is purged with blood, and …<u>WITHOUT THE SHEDDING OF BLOOD</u> **THERE CAN BE <u>NO</u> FORGIVENESS of sins.**"*

So if sorrow and regrets and confession, <u>instead of faith</u>, could get your sins forgiven, then Jesus didn't need to die!

Besides, *how would you ever know if you have regretted enough and spilled enough tears before God in sorrowful prayer **to deserve** forgiveness?*

Because then, you see, forgiveness *could be earned,* or it would be based *on FEELINGS instead of being based on <u>FAITH</u>.*

Listen, since God's truth has been made known as clearly as it has in the New Testament, *we can no longer afford to keep living by our short sighted, even blind, man-made religious opinions, traditional*

way of thinking, and sometimes outright speculations and superstitions.

Let me state again, *and make it as clear as day:* **If sorrow and regrets and confession can get your sins forgiven,** *then who needs <u>FAITH</u>?!*

I mean, if sorrow and regrets and confession can get your sins forgiven, *then who even needs Jesus?!*

I mean, if sorrow and regrets and confession can get your sins forgiven, *then Jesus didn't need to die!*

If mere sorrow and regrets and confession are all that is needed to get your sins forgiven, *then Jesus died in vain!*

If your sins are forgiven because of sorrow, regrets, and confession, *then how would you ever know that you have regretted enough, or felt bad enough, or how would you ever know that you have confessed enough times to finally deserve forgiveness?*

Listen, forgiveness from God cannot be based on feelings! Forgiveness from God cannot be earned!

If we <u>must</u> confess <u>all</u> our sins to be forgiven, *then what would happen if we forgot one?*

How on earth can we ever be sure that we had remembered them <u>all</u>?

And what would happen to the believer that died suddenly *before he could confess <u>just that one last sin</u>?*

Would that mean that the sacrifice of Jesus is now made void and that that person would now have to be punished *for that one sin* themselves, *or even be separated from God forever because of it?*

THIS *CANNOT* BE!

Let me ask you,

(and I am still talking in law terms, in legal terminology, because that seems to be the only way to get through to the logical thinkers out there, and hopefully I can then get past their logical mind into their hearts, so they can finally grasp these things in their spirit-man!)

Let me ask you this:

WHY IS GOD *JUST* IN FORGIVING OUR SINS?

Is it because we remembered to confess them?

Listen, in any court of law, *mere admission of guilt* <u>is not the basis of pardon</u>.

Release is only obtained after payment of penalty.

Would a Judge be just if he excused a murderer *because he just simply admitted to the crime?*

NO!

In the same way, God's JUSTICE in forgiving our sins *is founded upon the fact that Jesus has already paid the penalty for every sin* ...and not because of confession!

Does that mean we *should not feel sorrowful* when we discovered that we have *deceived ourselves* and *embraced the lie* and *given in* to sin's lure?

Does that mean we should *live in denial* and *should not admit it* when we are, in fact, guilty of *deceiving ourselves, embracing the lie, and giving in* to sin?

NO!!!

I am not saying that. I do not want you to misunderstand me here. *Godly sorrow* as a result of the impact of *"the word of TRUTH"* that sobers you up, *leads to true METANOIA,* a true paradigm shift, *a true renewal of the mind and <u>change</u> in thinking and behavior!*

So, *true Godly sorrow* aids the process of METANOIA. But I am not trying to speak to your *emotional* side of things right now. This subject *goes much deeper than emotions.* So I'm not *merely* talking about *sorrowful feelings* or *weeping and crying alone.* It goes much deeper!

Please bear with me and hear me out. I am trying to make a point.

METANOIA is based on TRUTH, not FEELINGS! METANOIA is birthed by THE TRUTH, by GOD'S TRUTH, and nothing else!

I am trying to get you to understand *the powerful, legal grounds* upon which God bases forgiveness. I am trying to give your faith firm ground *upon which to operate from.*

God's JUSTICE in forgiving our sins *is founded upon THE FACT that JESUS HAS ALREADY PAID THE PENALTY FOR EVERY SIN. It is not founded upon CONFESSION OF SIN! It is not founded upon FEELINGS of REGRET or SORROW!*

In the Old Covenant, **CONTINUAL SACRIFICES HAD TO BE OFFERED** *year by year* because it only PROPHETICALLY COVERED the sins of the people *for the previous year and it didn't even address the issue of future sins.*

It was an imperfect temporary covenant.

On the basis of these **CONTINUAL SACRIFICES** God *merely "**passed over** the sins **previously committed**".*

These sacrifices, **OFFERED CONTINUALLY,** were only *"shadows"* pointing towards a set date and a specific person: the Messiah, Jesus the Christ. ***THE ONE AND ONLY SACRIFICE,* the One who would come and be *THE PERFECT SACRIFICE,*** the One who would come and represent ***the fullness of time,*** the One who would come and pay for **all** those sins *"passed over"* **since the beginning of time** *and also for* **ALL** *THE SINS* **OF THE WHOLE WORLD THROUGHOUT ALL AGES TO COME!**

Remember, ***it is ONLY <u>on this basis of justice served</u>*** that sins are forgiven.

<u>**According to the Law**</u>**, God had to punish us for our sins. He had to uphold His justice. He could not just forget about our sins.**

That is why God made a personal appearance! That's why He came in Jesus *and personally took our judgment that we deserved* upon Himself, <u>*ONCE and for ALL*</u>.

(Forever, in other words, for all eternity! <u>ONCE and for ALL</u> also means: once, for every single individual)

God, personally, in and through Jesus, *dealt with our sins and its punishment once and for all.* **But more than that,** *He also dealt with <u>Sin itself</u>, as well as its fruit and all its ugly consequences and terrible affects upon our lives.*

He did it …once and for all!

He totally *justified us* **in every possible way, even in our existence,** *in our very being.*

He did it *all* **for us, once and for all,** *in order that He might be righteous in declaring us* **RIGHTEOUS! And in order that** *He may be justified* **in forgiving our sins!**

Romans 4:25,

"…He was delivered up because of our offenses and was raised from the dead because of our justification!"

Romans 5:1,

"…therefore, having been justified by faith, we now have peace with God through our Lord Jesus Christ!"

Listen, God believed in what was accomplished on that cross! Jesus was raised because of our justification!

"…therefore having been justified by faith,

By God's faith and by us embracing that faith, embracing what God the Father believes happened on that cross.)

"…having been justified by (that) *faith, we now have peace with God!"*

Colossians 2:13 says,

"…and you …He has made alive together with Jesus, having forgiven you all trespasses!"

So listen, *if there is still a need for more forgiveness then there must be YET <u>ANOTHER SACRIFICE</u> brought*, **because** *"there is no forgiveness of sins <u>without the shedding of blood</u>."*

You see, that would make Jesus' sacrifice *null and void.* **And that, my friend, can never happen because Jesus' sacrifice is** *"perpetually valid".*

What does *"perpetually valid"* **mean?**

It means that no future sin committed *can possibly invalidate the effect of Jesus' one and only sacrifice* **and therefore require** *an additional sacrifice.*

Nine times in the book of Hebrews from Chapter 7 through 10, **it is emphasized that Jesus died <u>ONCE</u>, FOR <u>ALL</u> SIN, FOR <u>ALL</u> MANKIND, FOR <u>ALL</u> TIME.**

If you are so inclined, *you can go read it for yourself:* Hebrews 7:11, 19, 27; 9:9, 12, 26-28; 10:1, 2, 10, 12, 14.

So, basically, when God stepped out of eternity into time in the incarnation, *to come and prove His love for us and to come and do away with sin, He took on flesh and blood and became a man.*

Now that man, Jesus Christ, was not only 100% God in the flesh, but He was also 100% Man. *He fully represented the fullness of both God and Man in one body!*

Thus, when He hung on that cross, He represented the whole human race! That means all of mankind from the beginning of time till the end of time ...Every single individual that has ever lived and will ever live was represented to the fullest!

So, as far as God is concerned, because Jesus fully represented the whole human race, every single individual, when He died, *we all died!* **And when He was raised from the dead,** *we were all raised from the dead to newness of life!*

God came and related to us by speaking the language of the Law, the only language we understood at that time, *and apparently, unfortunately, still today the only language many people understand.*

We, the guilty, were punished and died in Him!

But I want you to see that, not only did Jesus fully represent the whole human race, *but He also represented the fullness of God!*

Thus when He died, as far as God is concerned, *God Himself died!*

Bear with me, *hear me out now!*

What I mean by *"God Himself died"* is that **the concept of who God is, the God as He was with Man under the Law, and during that time of broken relationship** ...***that God died!***

That wasn't the true picture of who God really is anyway, *it wasn't the way He originally and still would prefer to relate to Man!*

Remember, *God is our Daddy, and God is love! But now because Man only understood the language of separation, the language of broken relationship, the language of the Law, He had to relate to Man as God the Judge!*

So, as far is God is concerned, *because Jesus both fully represented the human race and the fullness of the Godhead in*

bodily form, when He died, both God and Man died!

Our wrong concepts of who we really are and of who God really is all died when Jesus died!

Both the guilty and the Judge died at the same time, so that God could do away with the whole concept of the courtroom, and the whole language of Law ...and reintroduce in its place, the concept of a loving Father and His precious children!

In Jesus God reintroduced His own language, the original language and conversation we were designed for, the language of love, the language of romance!

Both God and Man died in one body, *and were raised to newness of Life, in Jesus Christ!*

You too were raised to newness of life in Jesus Christ!

In fact your whole relationship with God was raised to newness of life in Jesus Christ!

Chapter 2

Not an Inferior Redemption

So, getting back to law-language, Jesus died _ONCE_;

…*FOR _ALL_ SIN;*

…*FOR _ALL_ MANKIND;*

…*FOR _ALL_ TIME.*

Now, does this mean that *when I do blow it, **I now make Jesus a partaker of my sin?***

No, He will never condone sin!

He didn't come to lower God's standard and say, *'You know what guys, I know My Father always wanted ten out of ten, but it was so difficult and way too many of you find it too hard to pass the test, so now that I'm taking over the family business, don't worry about it. Say, five out of ten should do it, I'll just overlook the rest, it'll still be okay by Me!'*

He didn't come to say by His act of grace on the cross,

*'Go sin **a little less** now'*

or

*'Hey**, just don't do it so often**, and for God's sakes, **don't get caught doing it,** please. It'll make you and me both look bad!'*

No, that is not what He came to say!

He didn't come to introduce an inferior moral code, *a compromised set of rules, a sliding scale and degrading standard!*

You see, Jesus didn't come to do away with the law of the New Creation, or to ignore it, or compromise it, or water it down, or violate it.

By no means!

Righteousness, the life Jesus came to re-introduce to us, *that Christ-life, that original life we were designed for, and which is in us still,* it is not merely a hearsay-thing. *It's not fake;* it has nothing to do with being phony. *It is practical living that is faith inspired* and it gives new definition to the Law.

Jesus didn't come to undo the life portrayed in the Law of Moses; *He came to amplify it even more! He came to bring it into crystal clear focus! He came to be, and introduce, the very fulfillment of it!*

That life portrayed in the Law *merely prophetically pointed* to the life, *our life*, portrayed in Jesus!

He came to re-introduce to us that life, *that original design restored, that original life restored, our original life, which sets us free from sin, not free to sin!*

I say again,

He came to set us free from sin!

Chapter 3

Faith's Confession

Okay, let me get back to 1 John 1:9 now.

If **Jesus died _ONCE_,**

…**FOR _ALL_ SIN,**

…**FOR _ALL_ MANKIND,**

…**FOR _ALL_ TIME.**

…**does that mean we can now just rip 1 John 1:9 out of the Bible and throw it away?**

I mean, ***If Jesus paid for it all;***

…***If He came and shed His blood and dealt with sin's payment, once, and for _all_, for all time;***

…***If there remains no more sacrifice for sins;***

…***If He was the one and only Sacrifice,***

…***and there can be no other sacrifice ever again,***

*...I mean, **if there is no such teaching in the New Testament as** "...confession of sin,"*

*...**does that mean that there is no such thing as admission, and departure from sin,***

*...**does that mean that <u>confession in the face of sin</u> is not necessary under the New Covenant?***

*...**does that mean we can now rip 1 John 1:9 out of the Bible and throw it away?***

No, that would be absurd, wouldn't it!

Listen, if you have a problem, you might as well admit you have a problem, *so you can face it and deal with it!*

But you see, instead of ripping 1 John 1:9 out of our Bibles, *or simply going back to what we have always been wrongly taught,*

...the real question we should ask concerning, ***"if we confess our sin"* is:**

What is "confession" really?

*...**and how does it actually practically fit into my life as a Christian?***

Listen, we need to have a better understanding of the word ***"CONFESS"*** as used in the New Testament.

The word *"**CONFESS**"* or *"confession"* in the English language means: **To speak openly and freely as a result of a deep conviction of facts.**

So, *if we look at the context in 1 John* it is quite obvious that,

…yes, it is a fact that we messed up,

*…but there is **a greater fact** we need to consider;*

*…**those facts** we are to have **a deep conviction** about;*

*…**those facts we are to speak openly and freely** as a result of;*

*…**those facts** we are to be so bold about,*

*…**those facts** are **the forgiveness provided by Jesus' personal sacrifice and shed blood,***

*…**and also the deliverance from sin itself that He gave us** …by revealing the truth of redemption,*

*…by **revealing the truth of our original authentic design and true identity restored to us!***

We don't have to miss the mark and mess up anymore!

The real facts we are supposed to have <u>a deep conviction</u> about, *and be so bold and persuaded about,* is listed in the previous and following verses. It is listed in 1 John 1:8 & 10.

1 John 1:8 states,

*"…THE BLOOD OF JESUS… **CLEANSES US FROM <u>ALL</u> SIN…"***

…and 1 John 1:10 says that,

"…HE IS THE PROPITIATION,

(He, *in His very person,* is the Mediator; He is revealed to be *God and Man united in one body;*

…Because He *fully represents both* God and Man united in one body, He is therefore also *the personal means by whom* **God Himself <u>paid</u>**), *FOR **OUR** SINS,*

*…and not only for **our** sins,*

*…but **ALSO**,*

*…**FOR THE SINS OF THE WHOLE WORLD**"*

These are the <u>facts</u> 1 John 1:9 is sandwiched between.

<u>These</u> are the very <u>facts</u> in which there is <u>a deep conviction</u> expressed in our confession!

He reveals our innocence!

He reveals our freedom from sin!

He reveals our reconciliation and total oneness with the Father!

He reveals the TRUTH,

...which is our way of escape!

In other words, **that confession is worth nothing,** *unless it is a <u>faith</u>-confession!*

...a confession <u>that comes from faith</u>!

...that comes from <u>a deep conviction of redemption truth</u>,

...of redemption <u>realities</u>!

The word: *"**CONFESS,**"* in the original Greek, is derived from the word *'**HOMOLOGAO**',*

...which means,

...TO THINK AND SPEAK THE SAME THING;

...TO BE <u>UNITED</u> IN THOUGHT AND SPEECH WITH GOD HIMSELF.

It is a joining of the two words:

HOMO and **LOGAO** (or **LOGOS**)

HOMO – the same,

…and **LOGAO** – to speak,

Or **LOGOS** – the WORD;

…**the Word of Christ!**

…**the Word of His Grace!**

…**the Word of our Salvation in Christ!**

…**Redemption realities!**

…that **TRUTH;**

…REDEMPTION **TRUTH,**

…*the THOUGHTS of God;*

…*the OPINION of God;*

…*the CONCLUSION of God;*

…*the **FAITH** of God;*

…***what God has to say about us in Christ Jesus, in His incarnation and His work of redemption;***

…***what God believes happened on that cross, in that work of redemption;***

…***THAT is what confession is all about!***

…it's a conviction of the heart thing, concerning the success of redemption!

…it's a faith thing from beginning to end!

Thus the word: *"CONFESS"* can be translated as saying that **we should think and speak the same WORD;**

…that **we should think and speak the same thing as THE WORD;**

…that **we should think and speak** *the same thing as God does,*

…about our sins; about Jesus,

…about what God has to say to us, in His incarnation and work of redemption, concerning sin.

And what does God say to us *in the incarnation* **about sin?**

IT IS NOT PART OF OUR DESIGN!

IT DOESN'T BELONG!

What does God say to us *in redemption* **about sin?**

IT IS DEALT WITH!

In fact, to think and speak *the same thing as God does* **about our sins is the only**

basis for *embracing* forgiveness and *receiving freedom* from sin's hold.

We must walk **in <u>His</u> LIGHT,**

…not the light of the problem!

We must be conscious *of **His provision,***

…not conscious of the problem!

Walking in His Word; in His TRUTH, *you will know the truth of His provision,*

…not the truth of the extent of the problem!

The TRUTH of His Word *will set you free!*

Discussing your sin in detail with God <u>will not set you free;</u>

Discussing your sin in detail with God <u>will only put your focus on it, and put you in more and more bondage</u>!

Besides, why do we always think so easily, that we have the right to bore and disgust God, *with the gory details of our sins?*

…when He already knows about it!

You see, He already knows about it,

…but in the LIGHT of greater TRUTH;

...in the LIGHT of knowing a greater REALITY concerning us,

...He refuses to keep dwelling on our sin and its gory details!

Can you imagine what a miserable, depressing day God would have *if He were to meditate on the gory details of your sins all the time?*

Don't YOU now come, and be determined to depress God, and give God a bad day!

Ha... ha... ha...

I don't believe God *has any intentions* of having a bad day,

...I believe God is determined to have a good day,

...sometimes in spite of you,

Ha... ha... ha...

*...**because of what He knows to be TRUE about you!***

You see *focusing on* your sin will cause you to be caught up in your past,

*...***and in depression,***

*...**instead of being caught up in the LIGHT of the Lord's provision!***

We do not have to live in bondage to sin!

That is also why John says in 1 John 2:1,

*"My little children, **these things I write to you that you may not sin**,"*

*"And **IF** (…**not when,** but **IF**),*

*…**IF** anyone sins, **we do have an advocate who is <u>with</u> the Father,** Jesus Christ, the righteous one"*

He is <u>with</u> the Father!

He is <u>one with</u> the Father!

They are in *total agreement*!

Jesus is <u>with</u> the Father *on the issue of redemption realities!*

They *totally agree* about the work of redemption!

"…Jesus Christ, the righteous one …our advocate…"

That means; **He acts in a just manner and does everything <u>according to what is legal</u>.**

And He is not up there *trying to constantly get you out of trouble before God …by arguing in your favor before the Judge of the universe,*

No, He is <u>one with</u> the Father, *they are in total agreement!*

If Jesus is arguing any *legal matters* …**it is not before God, our Father,**

…*it is before you, <u>to fully persuade you</u>!*

If Jesus is arguing any *legal matters* …**it is not before the eternal unchanging Almighty God, who cannot plan and then fail, who decrees a thing and it is so,**

…*as if God has you still in test phase and on probation, before He will make His mind up about you.*

No, He has *already made up His mind about you!*

He is just *waiting on you,*

…*and <u>working on influencing you</u>,*

…*with HIS ETERNAL TRUTH,*

…*so you may get it through your thick skull, and grasp it finally!*

…*so you may know and believe what He is already persuaded about!*

...*He is persuaded about how free and whole you already are!*

Sin is dealt with, and you are free from sin itself!

…so, you can be free NOW!

…if you'd only EMBRACE that reality, and BELIEVE it!

Sin is dealt with, and you are free from sin itself!

That is what God is <u>persuaded about</u> already!

God wants YOU <u>to be persuaded</u> in the same thing;

…that Sin is dealt with,

…and you are free from sin <u>already</u>!

If the enemy *successfully tempts you* **into some alternative fulfillment,**

…<u>simply realize</u>, you don't have to sit there in condemnation and sin-consciousness, and self-loathing!

<u>Realize</u>, you have been lied to;

<u>Realize</u> you have been deceived;

Get back to GOD's ETERNAL TRUTH;

Get back into the LIGHT of His provision!

BECAUSE,

*"**He** was **wounded** for **our** transgressions;*

*…**He** was **bruised** for **our** iniquities.*

*…The **chastisement** <u>for our peace</u>,*

*…came upon **Him**,*

*…and by **His** stripes,*

*…<u>**our healing (our wholeness of being) was bought and paid for**</u>"*

Romans 6:14,

*"For sin **shall not be** your master …**because you are** … **under grace**"*

…because God in His grace totally set you free, and made you whole!

…and that TRUTH;

…that REALITY,

*…*NOW *empowers you* to defeat sin,

*…<u>**and stay free**</u> from its influence,*

*…<u>**refusing**</u> to come under its spell; its illusion …its temporary entertainment of deception and empty lies!*

*…<u>**refusing**</u> to give into SIN!*

Listen, *we cannot prefer SIN to God's presence!*

We are fools indeed *if we do so!*

Resist **the devil,**

…steadfast in the FAITH,

…steadfast in the TRUTH,

…steadfast in FAITH,

…and God will restore *YOUR RIGHTEOUSNESS.*

…He will restore *YOUR FREEDOM.*

Realize **that it's the Father's total heart's desire** <u>to sustain you</u> *in intimate fellowship;*

…<u>to sustain intimacy</u> with YOU!

If your dearly beloved son, your precious little boy, disappoints you, do you now *wipe him off the face of the earth?*

…or, wipe him out of your heart and out of your memory?

…or do you seek restoration?

Well, **God is the same!**

God Seeks restoration!

(*…*unless of course you are an abusive unfit father to your kids; *in which case you have gotten so far lost* that you won't have a clue what I'm talking about, and **God won't be the same way you are.**)

So, whether it is your heart or not, it is the heart of God *to sustain* <u>**unbroken intimacy with YOU**</u>**!**

*…**and thereby to reach your neighbor,***

*…**as you talk with them, and interact with them, out of that inner-court of uninterrupted fellowship with God.***

Hebrews 10:19-22

19 *"Therefore, brethren,* **since we have confidence to enter the very presence of God by the blood of Jesus***"*

20 *"…**by the new and living way which He opened for us** through the curtain, that is,* **through** *(the tearing of; or the laying down of) His flesh,* **(through His death in the flesh)***,"*

21 *"…and since we have such a great High Priest over the house of God,"*

22 *"…let us draw near* **with a true heart** *and* **in full assurance of faith***,"*

*"...with <u>our hearts sprinkled clean from **an evil conscience**</u>"*

(...a conscience full of darkness, ignorance, unbelief and lies and deception. *"Paneros"* is the word in the Greek for *evil,* and it meas: Hardship, labors, toil, annoyances and frustration. Thus it speaks of a conscience ruled by condemnation, guilt and shame because of your own religious works-mentality.)

"...and our bodies washed (cleansed, made presentable, qualified, set free) *...with pure water."*

...Set free and made acceptable by the water of the Word; by the water of Redemption realities; by the water of GOD's ETERNAL TRUTH; by the water of His Spirit influence in that TRUTH; *by the water of His love for us!*

You see the secret of success lies in *walking in the LIGHT!*

...in the same LIGHT,

*"...<u>**as He is in the light**</u>."*

...walking in THAT light!

In other words,

...knowing and believing and embracing HIS TRUTH!

...knowing and believing and embracing HIS LOVE!

...knowing and believing and embracing that REALITY,

...redemption REALITIES!

...the way God sees it and KNOWS it to be!

He is CONSCIOUS of His Son's successful achievement on our behalf,

...so let us also be!

That is God's REALITY!

...and everything outside of *that,*

...or that does not bring *THAT* into consideration,

...and does not therefore EMPHASIZE it,

<u>*...is a rotten LIE*</u>!

There is nothing that can *convince you* of your ABSOLUTE INNOCENCE more than the <u>REALIZATION</u> that it has *nothing* to do with your own attempts and efforts *to be holy!*

There is nothing that can *convince you* of your ABSOLUTE INNOCENCE more than the <u>REALIZATION</u> that it has *everything* to do with *the one event* in which God completely and forever *dealt with EVERYTHING that stood between us and Him!*

Chapter 4

Real Freedom from Addiction

'How do you actually get free from an addiction or a bad habit, like smoking for instance, brother Rudi?'

Listen, Jesus did not go down into the lowest parts of the earth on a sightseeing tour. *He was on a rescuing mission!*

"He led us (humanity) *as trophies in his triumphant procession on high."*
- Ephesians 4:8

Jesus didn't just solve your problem by waving a magic wand from afar. **He actually entered into the middle of the conflict. He literally stepped into the domain of contradiction, He entered into our hell. In fact, He went beyond that. He entered into hell itself,** *faced death itself, and there He absolutely conquered EVERYTHNG that stood between us and Him.*

He entered into frail humanity, into a flesh and blood body, *and redeemed its original purpose, not just by His TRUTH, but* *literally by His very LIFE within us.* By His eternal resurrection LIFE within us;

…that He released,

…and gave to us,

…after His ascension,

…to abide within us!

By that resurrection LIFE, that LIFE, that FAITH-ENERGY, that spirit energy, that Spirit, that Holy Spirit, He conquers all contradiction and conflict within us!

By His Spirit of Truth within us, by His very LIFE within us, He causes us to no longer walk out duality, to no longer walk out ambivalence towards Father God and His Truth about us.

We no longer walk in a dual, *confused* expression, but we can and do NOW walk in confident, firm persuasion *of our freedom,* of who we REALY ARE IN CHRIST *in UNION WITH HIM,* GOD'S MASTERPIECE!

1 John 3:9 says,

"No one born (begotten) *of God* [deliberately, knowingly, and habitually] *practices sin …for God's nature abides in him* [His principle of LIFE, the Divine SPERM …remains permanently within him]*"*

Note that **He is talking about** *"...the Word of TRUTH."* **That's God's sperm, that very image and likeness of God within us and** *that very LIFE FORCE of God's SPIRIT that remains permanently within us.*

"...God's nature abides in him [His principle of LIFE, the Divine SPERM remains permanently within him];

...and he cannot practice sinning, because he is born (begotten) *of God."*
— Amplified Version

1 John 3:8-10 in the Breath of Life Translation says it this way,

8 *"**Being trapped in a continual cycle of sin has its origin in believing false accusations;***

...that which opposes that ultimate REALITY IN HIM is the source of continually missing the mark,

*(...i.e. **living outside of what you were designed for**)."*

*"**Sin is opposing REALITY.***

This opposition has NO REAL EXISTANCE;

*...**it only exists in its OPPOSITION TO REALITY**..."*

The words *"false accusation"* or **DIABOLOS** in the original language is derived from *'opponent'* or *'accuse.'* Thus **to sin is to believe and act in accordance with this false accusation**.

1 John 3:8-10,

8 *"...For this very purpose the Son of God revealed HIS REALITY;*

...to show the futility of that which opposes THAT REALITY;

...thereby dissolving its affect."

9 *"Everything born of God and proceeding from Him cannot continue to oppose Him, for His seed is more enduring than the opposition. God is not the source of that which opposes Him."*

10 *"In this it is obvious what proceeds from God and what proceeds from that which opposes Him;*

...Acting contrary to your innocence, does not originate in God;

...neither is anything that would cause you to be unloving to those who have the same origin in Him as you."

Listen, my friend, *the same Jesus that overcame every temptation, that same*

Spirit that even raised Him from the dead, IS ALIVE AND ACTIVE IN YOU, ready to strengthen and deliver you!

No bad habits or addictions of any kind need to rule over you anymore. <u>There is ONE LORD</u>!

*"**Consider yourself dead to sin** (any harmful thought pattern or habit or addiction) **and alive to God.**"*

- Romans 6:10-15

The key to your victory is not in your own self-discipline, *but<u> in the accuracy of your insight</u>*! HIS DEATH SETTLED <u>EVEN THIS MATTER</u>!

Romans 6:10-14,

10 *"**For by the death He died,** He died to sin [ending His relation to it] once and for all;*

…and the life that He lives, He is living to God [in unbroken union and fellowship with Him]."

11 *"**Even so (or just so), consider yourself also dead to sin, and your relation and constant reference to it, broken;***

…consider yourself rather, alive to God [living in uninterrupted union and fellowship with Him] in Christ Jesus."

12 "**Let not sin <u>therefore</u> rule as king in your mortal** (natural) **bodies;**

…to make you yield to its cravings and be subject to its lusts and evil passions (and resulting sins);"

Listen, Sin always wants to use your body to express itself.

BUT, *in the light of redemption REALITIES, in the light of your living union with Christ Jesus and Father God through that abiding FAITH-LIFE, that abiding LIFE source, through that abiding Spirit of Truth, that abiding Spirit of LIFE, that abiding SPIRIT, that abiding TRUTH and POWER ...In the light of that LIVING Jesus within you, that CHRIST you can rely on, in the light of that REALITY, in the light of all that:*

12 "**Let not sin <u>therefore</u> rule as king in your mortal** (natural) **bodies…"**

13 "**Do not continue offering or yielding your bodily members [and faculties] to sin;**

…as instruments (tools) of wickedness;

…but rather, offer and yield yourselves to God as though you have been raised from the dead to [perpetual] LIFE;

…offer your bodily members [and faculties] to God;

...presenting them as instruments of righteousness!"

14 *"For sin shall not [any longer] exert dominion over you;*

*...**SINCE NOW YOU ARE** no longer under the Law [as slaves], but **under grace** [as subjects of God's favor and mercy]."*
- Amplified Version

14 *"For sin shall not [any longer] exert dominion over you;*

*...**SINCE NOW YOU ARE** under GRACE, under THAT influence and power, under the influence of God's mercy, under the influence of GOD's TRUTH and of GOD's POWER!*

*'So, brother Rudi, I don't TRY to quit? **I just SIMPLY REALIZE** that I'm **REALLY NOT** IN BONDAGE?'*

'Is that it? Is it that simple?'

YES! That is it! IT IS NOT ROCKET SCIENCE! EVEN A CHILD CAN GRASP IT!

You simply have to *REALIZE* that you are REALLY NOT IN BONDAGE!

THEN GO AHEAD AND *EMBRACE THAT REALITY FULLY*!

Look, all of Romans 5-8 is such powerful revelation, *and for those who get it,* it is an absolute MIND-BENDER!

Paul's CONCLUTION is:

You are ALIVE!

Many get stuck on the Scripture that says, *"It's not I who live, but Christ who lives in me",* **and they feel as though they are not quite good enough to co-live with Him.**

Herein is the mind-bender: *How can you be in the grave, and ALIVE in Him, at the same time?*

It was <u>the stained you</u> that was crucified with Him. *But don't miss the **CONCLUSION** of what Romans 6 really says.* **Yes, we DIED with Him, BUT** *it also clearly lays out* **that,**

*"**WE** WERE ALSO **RAISED UP** WITH HIM;*

…and are now <u>ALIVE</u> in Him."

He did not BRING YOU FORTH into this world *to simply control your every move.* He did not place you in your mother's womb, *inside a body formed and fashioned **just for YOU, so that you could DANCE AND PERFORM at the end of His puppet strings, just existing to entertain His every desire!***

No, no, no!

He brought you into existence *to LIVE!*

Today, you are *FREE!*

Today, *consider doing life WITH Him,* verses trying your best *to live life FOR Him* and feeling like you are moving about *under strict orders! Feeling like you never qualify and measure up!*

Listen, that kind of stifling, religious belief-system is not so much Good News.

The Good News is:

You are ALIVE in Him!

It is great to consider the fact that *YOU are actually a part of this whole deal! This whole newness of life, this whole thing of giving expression to LIFE,* not some fake life, a life that is dying or dead, but *a real LIFE,* a CELEBRATION of *LIFE,* a life of FREEDOM in Him, *of JOY and of LOVE, and ENJOYMENT of your TRUE FREE self,* of who you REALLY are in Him, *and of others* CELEBRATING and promoting *who they REALLY are in Him!*

*The truth is **God likes your take on LIFE!***

So LIVE IT!

I'm not talking about the flesh life, living for the lusts of the flesh, *but the Spirit LIFE!*

God likes your take on that LIFE, **on <u>LIFE</u> ITSELF!**

LIVE IT FREE and LARGE!

BOLD and BEAUTIFUL!

And definitely OUTSIDE THOSE RESTRICTIVE LEGALISTIC RELIGIOUS LINES! That DEATH-TRAP OF LAW!

Chapter 5

Freedom Realized!

I am including my friend Andre Rabe's article on CONFESSION *because I know it might just be the key to help some of you unlock this whole thing, this FREEDOM FROM SIN REALITY!*

CONFESSION – by Andre Rabe

A chapter from the booklet Metanoia and Repentance http://www.amazon.com/Metania-Repentance-Questions-Answers-ebook/dp/B00721617E/

One subject that is normally closely connected to repentance is confession.

John starts off this letter with the overwhelming awareness of fellowship with God: *a fellowship that is tangible.*

In 1 John 1:6 he starts addressing a situation in which some have reduced this message and its implications to less than what it really is.

"…if we say we are intimate with Him, but continue to live in darkness, we deceive

ourselves. ***This truth is made to be lived!****"*
(Breath of Life Translation)[1]

Some heard the message to the extent that they could *'talk'* the message, but it did not affect their *'walk'*. Which is just a figure of speech to say that the way they lived remained in darkness.

Here, and throughout this letter, John strongly argues that the implications of this message are not just theoretical! It doesn't just give you a new way of thinking and speaking. **The implications of accurately understanding this message <u>is evident in every detail of your life</u>,** *especially in how you relate to people.*

Verse 7,

"But if we allow this light to become the reality we live in, the same reality He lives in, it results in uninterrupted enjoyment of one another, and the blood of Jesus Christ constantly cleanses us from every attempt to draw us back into a lesser reality *(missing the mark)."*

What is the value of all you believe *if it does not bring you to a place of tangible interaction with God and enjoyment of people?*

---
[1] Portions of this translation is available at
http://AlwaysLoved.net

True enlightenment is not based on how convincingly you can argue that you are right, but it is made evident in *'uninterrupted enjoyment of one another'*.

Some have taken verse 8 out of context to say that *we can never be free from sin.*

"…if we say that we have no sin, we deceive ourselves, and the truth is not in us." (1 John 1:8 NKJV)

However, *John is addressing the same people or the same situation as in verse 6.*

Verse 6 said,

*"…if we say we are intimate with Him, **but** continue to live in darkness…"*

Can we say that we are intimate with Him?

Yes!

John just said it himself in Verse 3!

Can we say that we are without sin?

Yes!

"…The blood of Jesus cleanses us continually…"

But don't just say that you are without sin *while you still continue to live in darkness.*

John addresses people who simply *'confesses'* these words, who continue to *say* they agree with the gospel message, with the truth of it, **but they don't mean it!**

They *'confess'* with their mouth, **they say they believe, but then continues in a lifestyle that John later described as hateful.**

To continue in a lifestyle of sin while simply confessing that you have no sin *is idiotic.*

God has made available His reality, His Word, and His whole world! Why continue in a lesser reality, *in a life that is less than His original plan?* Authentic life is available, *why continue in a fake existence?*

If you find yourself still enslaved to sin, Verse 9 gives such clear guidance **in *breaking with it once and for all.*** The word we translated *"confession"* is HOMOLOGEO, and is made up of two base words, namely:

1) HOMOU, Genitive case of HOMOS (the same) as adverb; at the same place or time: - together.

And

2) LOGOS, Something said (including the thought); by implication a topic (subject of discourse), also reasoning (the mental faculty) or motive; by extension a computation;

specifically (with the article in John) the Divine Expression (that is, Christ).

To confess is more than acknowledging sin's existence. To confess sin is to say the same (HOMOU) thing about sin as God says about it. It is to come into agreement with the LOGOS of God, the logic of God, *which is most accurately displayed in the Word made flesh; Jesus Christ.*

What does God say about sin?

Jesus demonstrated that sin is not something that our Father tolerates, and puts up with. No, *He eradicated it at the greatest cost.* Jesus did not come to lower the standard.

Why is He so intolerant of sin? **Because He does not want to settle for a lesser quality of friendship, *a lesser intimacy than what is possible.* The deeds of sin are manifestations of the mindset of sin. The mindset of sin accepts a lesser reality about ourselves and about God. God designed Man for perfect harmony, *perfect union!* God designed Man in a place of absolute innocence.**

Sin is to accommodate less than His persuasion, to accommodate distance!

What else does God say about sin?

It is dealt with!

God was in Christ, reconciling the world to Himself, not holding their trespasses against them.

We could not deal with Sin ourselves. The Law system gave us all the opportunity we needed to prove that through our own efforts we could live up to God's standard. **But over and over again we proved that we could not consistently do so.**

So God came and did for us what we could not do for ourselves. He conquered Sin in the flesh and gave us His own victorious life.[2]

God did not make a mistake when He gave the Law, neither was He unaware that the Law would in itself not solve the problem of separation. He knew and purposely designed the Law in such a way that it would intensify the conflict, that it would reveal the problem for what it really was and reveal Man's impotence to solve the problem by himself. He designed this environment of conflict, a conflict that was working its way towards a climax!

Under the Law, Man and God never met face to face. Instead of direct contact with God, the Law became the intermediary by which Man related to God, based on a knowledge of good

---
2 Romans 8:3

and evil, right and wrong. **The Law maintained the distance between God and Man,** *and in so doing prolonged and intensified the conflict.*

Although the Law was not designed to solve the problem of separation, *it was designed to reveal and amplify the problem.* The Law revealed another law or government. Paul says that under the Law he discovered another law or government at work within him.

"...for I delight in the law of God according to the inward man.

...But I see another law at work in my members;

...warring against the law of my mind;

...and bringing me into captivity to the law of sin which is at work in my members."[3]

The experience of Man under the Law is that *there is a stronger influence at work in Man that forces him to live contrary to what he knows is right.*

The flesh became the domain of Sin, and Man by himself was helpless to change the situation.

And so Paul continues in Verse 23,

---

[3] Romans 7:21, 22

"O wretched man that I am! Who will deliver me from this body of death? I thank God – through Jesus Christ our Lord!"

The fullness of time was drawing near in which the final judgment upon sin and self-righteousness would be completed.

"But when the fullness of the time had come;

…God sent forth His Son;

…born of a woman;

…born under the law;

…to redeem those who were under the law;

…that we might receive the adoption as sons."[4]

God was preparing to enter the domain of Sin – *flesh*. He was preparing to enter the strong man's house, bind him and spoil his goods.

*"…**for what the law was powerless to do** because it was weakened by the flesh;*

*…**God did;***

…by sending His own Son in the likeness of sinful flesh, to be a sin offering. And so he condemned sin in the flesh."[5]

---

4 Galatians 4:4, 5
5 Romans 8:3

He came to take back every part of humanity that came from Him and that He created, *including flesh!*

So what does God say about sin?

He conquered it!

It no longer has any right to rule in your body!

Now say to sin what God says to it,

"It is over. You (sin) are no longer worth my attention!"

"From now on my life is a glorious adventure occupied with God and HIS REALITY!"

1 John 1:9-2:2,

"But rather through aligning ourselves with the logic of God, agreeing with Him, we deal with sin with this clear declaration:

He is faithful;

He is just;

He forgives us;

…cleansing us from anything that tries to contaminate our blameless innocence!"

*Confession of sin is not the act in which we tell God about our sin, but the act **in which we tell sin about our God**.*

1 John 1:10,

*"If we deny that there was ever a problem, **we deny the very One who came to fix things.**"*

That's obviously not entirely true. **We may remain outside of the influence and freedom He came to bring, our lives remain broken,** *but whether we deny Him or not,* **He still came and He fixed things.**

So whether we try to deny that there is a problem, or that there ever was a problem, *makes no difference <u>when it comes to truth</u>.*

It doesn't change *the truth of what happened!* **He came and fixed things, and our denying Him, or our denying of the facts of redemption, or even denying the fact that we have a problem and refusing to deal with it,** *doesn't change REALITY.* **It doesn't change the REALITY of what He did; it only robs us from experiencing that liberty!**

What happened in Him on our behalf IS REALITY!

1 John 2:1,

*"My precious little ones let me make this clear: **you don't have to sin!***

And if anyone does fall short, we have an advocate with the Father, Jesus Christ the Righteous."

Our advocate has indisputable evidence that your debt has been paid. In His own righteous person, He represents your innocence!

**"*He is Himself the atonement for our sin;*

…and not for ours only;

…but for the whole world!"**

In closing, I urge you to get yourself a copy of *"The Mirror Bible"* available online at www.Amazon.com and several other book sellers. It is the best paraphrased version of the New Testament Scriptures, translated from the original Greek, that I have ever read.

If you want me or someone a part of our team to come to where you are, anywhere in the world, and give a talk or teach you and some of your friends about the gospel message and redemption realities, simply contact us at www.LivingWordIntl.com. Or you can always find me on Facebook.

If you have been helped, or your perspective on life has changed, as a result of reading this book, please get in touch with me and let me know.

I would love to share your joy, so that my joy in writing this book may be full!

"That which was from the beginning,

which we have heard **(with our spiritual ears)**, which we have seen **(with our spiritual eyes)**, which we have looked upon **(beheld, focused our attention upon)**, and which our hands have also handled **(which we have also experienced)**,

concerning the Word of life, we declare to you, **that <u>you also</u> may have this fellowship <u>with us</u>; and <u>truly our fellowship is with the Father</u> <u>and with His Son Jesus Christ.</u>** And these things we write to you **that your joy may be full."**
— 1John 1:1-4

About The Author

Rudi & Carmen Louw together oversee: Living Word International.

They also travel and minister both locally and internationally.

Rudi was born and raised in the country of South Africa while Carmen grew up in Cortland, New York.

They function in the ministry of reconciliation (2Corinthians 5:18-21) and flow strongly with the Holy Spirit and His anointing to teach, preach, prophecy, heal *and whatever is needed to touch people's lives* **with the reality of God's love and power.**

God has given them keen insight into what He has to say to mankind in the work of redemption, *concerning the revelation of, and restoration of, **humanity's true identity**,* and therefore they emphasize THE GOSPEL, IN CHRIST REALITIES, the GRACE of God, the WORD OF RIGHTEOUSNESS, *and all such eternal truths **essential to salvation and living of the CHRIST-LIFE.***

They have been granted this wisdom and revelation into the knowledge of God by the Spirit of Truth; by the resurrected Spirit of Jesus Christ Himself, *to establish and strengthen believers **in THE FAITH OF GOD, and to activate them in ministering to others.***

Not only are people set free from the poison and bondage of sin, condemnation and all kinds of intimidation, (upheld, strengthened and reinforced by age old religious ideas born out of ignorance and deception,) *but many are brought into a closer more intimate relationship with Father God, **as Daddy**, through accurate teaching, and unveiling of the gospel message, prophetic words, healings and miracles.*

Rudi & Carmen are closely knitted together with many other effective Christians, church fellowships, and groups of believers *who share the same revelation and passion to impart the truth of the gospel to others, **so as to impact and transform the world we live in with the LOVE and POWER of God.***

www.ingramcontent.com/pod-product-compliance
Lightning Source LLC
Chambersburg PA
CBHW072023060426
42449CB00034B/1881